A WOMAN WHO

A WOMAN WHO

Drawings by

Rebecca Miller

Published by Bloomsbury, New York and London
Distributed to the trade by Holtzbrinck Publishers

Library of Congress Cataloging-in-Publication Data has been applied for.

ISBN 1-58234-353-5

First U.S. Edition 2003

1 3 5 7 9 10 8 6 4 2

Printed in Mexico

For Daniel, Ronan, Cashel, and Dad

Introduction

I made the first "Woman Who" drawing by accident. It was 1990, and I was sitting for a photographic portrait by my friend Robert Younger. Robert had asked each of his subjects to "conceal what reveals you most" on their faces with masking tape. I dutifully went into the bathroom and taped up my eyes, a choice I began to regret almost instantly.

After twenty minutes of excruciating boredom sitting on a stool in the dark while Robert clicked away, I asked for a pad of paper and a pen. And I said to Robert, tell me what to draw. And he said, "A woman who doesn't know the meaning of the word 'awkward.'" So, imagining where the pen was on the page, I drew a woman wearing a dress so short it reveals the fact that she forgot to wear underwear – and yet she's perfectly happy! When I took off the blindfold I was surprised to see a coherent drawing there, a drawing that made us both laugh. So, for the rest of the afternoon, and for days after, I got my friends to give me "Woman Who" subjects to draw. I would look up at the ceiling, imagine myself as the character in her dilemma, and draw – on napkins, scrap paper, the backs of paper menus. The rule was, I had to write the subject down first, and when I looked down, I was finished.

Not all the drawings work, of course. At times I go right off the page. At times they are incoherent, or emotionally flat. The truth is, the drawings only work when I succeed in becoming the woman in the drawing in my own head – I need to get under her skin, feel what she feels. Though I have tried, I have never been able to come close to the same effect by sight drawing.

Over the years, I have continued to make "A Woman Who" drawings whenever I feel the urge, making up my own captions and following the original rules. Up until now, I have made them for myself or my friends, scattering them in notebooks and journals. I've collected my favorites into this book – I hope you enjoy them.

A WOMAN WHO IS UNBELIEVABLY BORED

A WOMAN WHO AIMS TO PLEASE

A WOMAN WHO IS BEGINNING TO WONDER
IF SHE ISN'T SOME SORT OF LOW · GRADE
NYMPHOMANIAC

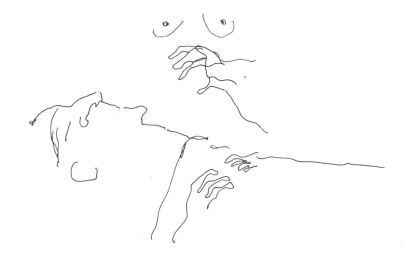

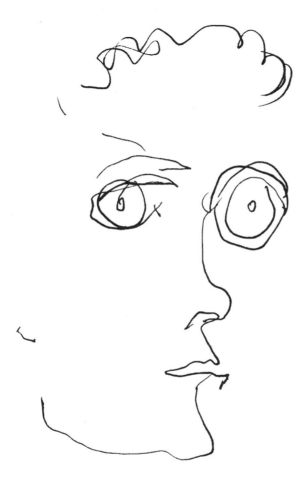

A WOMAN WHO GETS CONFESSIONAL WHEN SHE DRINKS

A WOMAN WHO WAS OKAY A SECOND AGO

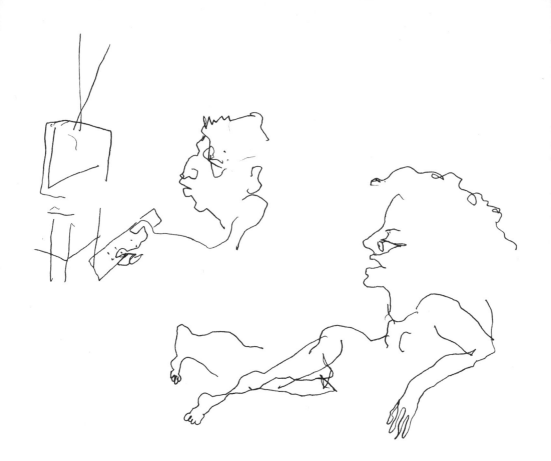

A WOMAN WHO WOULD LIKE SOME ATTENTION
BUT ISN'T SURE HOW TO GET IT IN A SUBTLE WAY

A WOMAN WHO SECRETLY PRETENDS SHE'S A
GEISHA WHEN GOING OUT ON DATES

A WOMAN WHO GOES TO PARTIES JUST SO SHE CAN SNIFF THE CHEESE.

A WOMAN WHO JUST WANTS TO GIVE AND GIVE AND GIVE

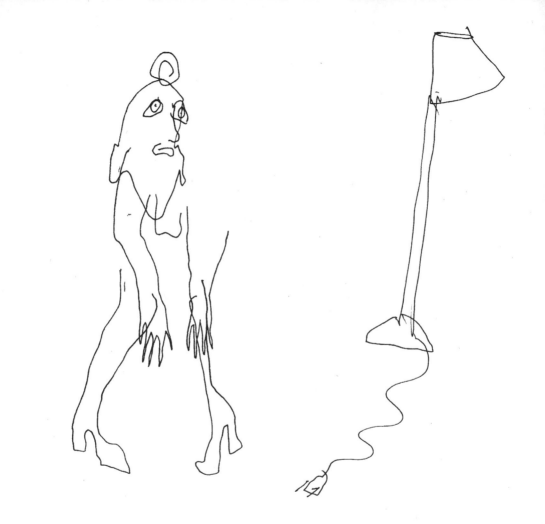

A WOMAN WHO FEELS SHE MAY HAVE CHOSEN THE WRONG LAMP

A WOMAN WHO IS COMING TO REALIZE SHE IS A
VERY ANGRY PERSON

A WOMAN WHO IS INTIMIDATED BY HER MOTHER'S HOSTESSING SKILLS

A WOMAN WHO JUST SPENT AN HOUR LOOKING AT A FASHION MAGAZINE AND NOW SHE'S DISCOURAGED

A WOMAN WHO FEELS BETTER WITH HER BLUE JEANS ON

A WOMAN WHO HAS SO MANY THINGS TO DO THAT SHE CAN'T BRING HERSELF TO DO ANY OF THEM

A WOMAN WHO IS REALLY SLEEPY BUT ISN'T ALLOWED
TO TAKE A NAP

A WOMAN WHOSE DAYS JUST SEEM TO GO ON FOREVER

A WOMAN WHO CAN'T STOP SMILING AND IT'S REALLY STARTING TO GET HER DOWN

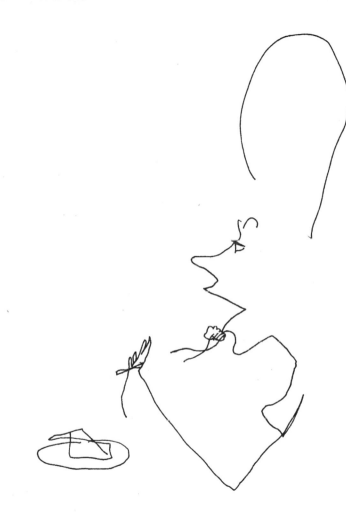

A WOMAN WHO PRIDES HERSELF ON HER TIDY EATING HABITS

A WOMAN WHO HAS AN INEXPLICABLE DESIRE TO LEARN HOW TO COOK

A WOMAN WHO SUDDENLY REALIZES SHE IS REALLY HAPPY

A WOMAN WHO IS PISSED OFF BECAUSE SHE CAN NEVER STAY
IN A BAD MOOD FOR MORE THAN FIFTEEN MINUTES

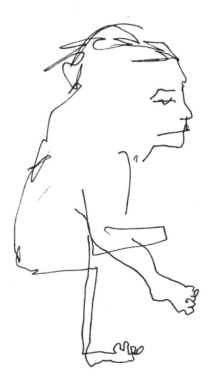

A WOMAN WHO LOVES TO SUFFER

A WOMAN WHO JUST MENTIONED LIVING TOGETHER A LITTLE TOO EARLY AND DIDN'T GET A VERY POSITIVE RESPONSE

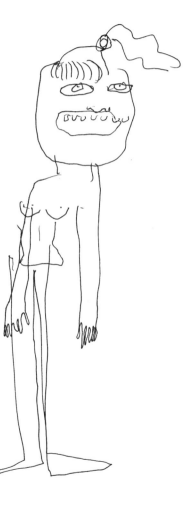

A WOMAN WHO HAS DECIDED TO BECOME BLASÉ FOR TACTICAL REASONS

A WOMAN WHO FINALLY OWNS HER RAGE
(AND NOW SHE'S WONDERING WHAT THE NEXT STEP IS)

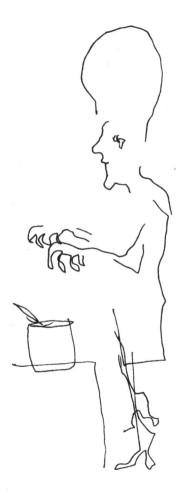

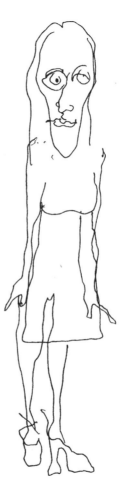

A WOMAN WHO IS GOING OUT FOR THE FIRST TIME SINCE SHE STARTED
TRANSLATING ALL OF PLOTINUS INTO SWEDISH

A WOMAN WHO IS FEELING SO SERENE THAT SHE
CAN BARELY SPEAK

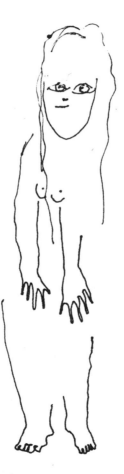

A WOMAN WHO IS SICK OF WHAT SHE HAS BUT ALSO FEARS LOSING IT

A WOMAN WHO WOULD RATHER BE LIVING IN NEW YORK

A WOMAN WHO DOESN'T KNOW WHAT SHE WANTS
AND IT'S GETTING LATE

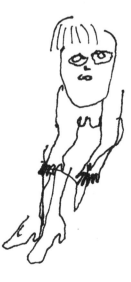

A WOMAN WHO PRIDES HERSELF ON BEING EXTREMELY FRANK

A WOMAN WHO REALIZES SHE IS GETTING A LITTLE BIT FAT, BUT SHE'S TRYING NOT TO LET IT BOTHER HER

A WOMAN WHO LOVES TO BE LOVED SO MUCH THAT SHE'S DRIVING
EVERYBODY CRAZY

A WOMAN WHO IS BEGINNING TO WISH THAT SHE HADN'T
COME TO THIS PARTY

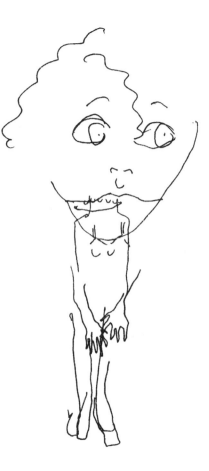

A WOMAN WHO JUST WORKED OUT THAT SHE AND HER HUSBAND
MADE LOVE TEN TIMES LAST YEAR AND SHE'S TRYING TO PUT
A POSITIVE SPIN ON IT

A WOMAN WHO FINALLY GETS TO WORK AND IS HORRIFIED TO FIND
THAT SHE HAS NOTHING TO SAY

A WOMAN WHO IS STRANGELY UNNERVING

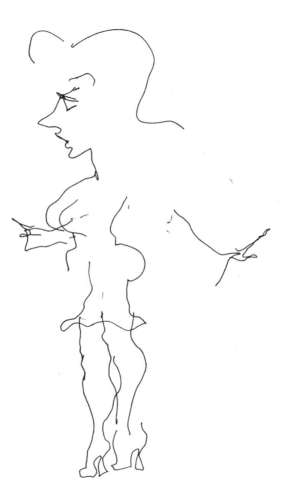

A WOMAN WHO OTHER WOMEN WISH WOULDN'T COME TO THE PARTIE.

A WOMAN WHO SUDDENLY WISHES SHE HAD LONG HAIR

A WOMAN WHO DOESN'T KNOW THE MEANING OF THE WORD "AWKWARD"

A WOMAN WHO HAS BEEN IN ANALYSIS FOR TEN YEARS AND
THINKS SHE KNOWS THE REAL REASONS FOR EVERYBODY'S ACTIONS

A WOMAN WHO IS HAVING VIOLENT FEELINGS TOWARD HER DINNER GUESTS

A WOMAN WHO SUDDENLY REALIZES THE MAN SHE LOVES ISN'T
AS SMART AS SHE THOUGHT HE WAS

A WOMAN WHO MAKES LOVE TO HER HUSBAND WILDLY IN HER
SLEEP AND SURPRISES HIM

A WOMAN WHOSE BABY JUST WOKE UP AT THREE O'CLOCK
IN THE MORNING

A WOMAN WHO JUST GOT WHAT SHE ALWAYS WANTED AND SUDDENLY
IT DOESN'T SEEM SO GREAT ANYMORE

A WOMAN WHO JUST REALIZED SHE LOST HER PERSONALITY
SOMEWHERE ALONG THE LINE

A WOMAN WHO WANTS TO GO TO SOMEONE'S HOUSE

A WOMAN WHO HAS A SECRET DESIRE TO PUNCTURE
HER HUSBAND'S ANKLES

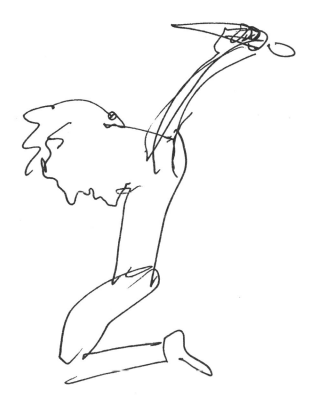

A WOMAN WHO KILLS HER HUSBAND IN HER SLEEP BECAUSE

OF WHAT SHE'S DISCOVERED ABOUT HIM ON OTHER OCCASIONS

IN HER SLEEP

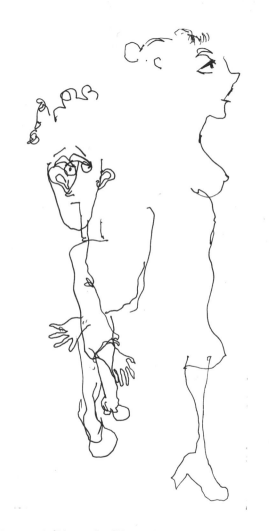

A   WOMAN   WHO IS THINKING OF KILLING HERSELF FOR SPITE

A WOMAN WHO IS TRYING TO REMAIN CALM

A WOMAN WHO IS STARTING TO LOOK LIKE HER MOTHER

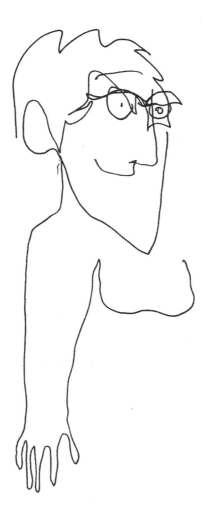

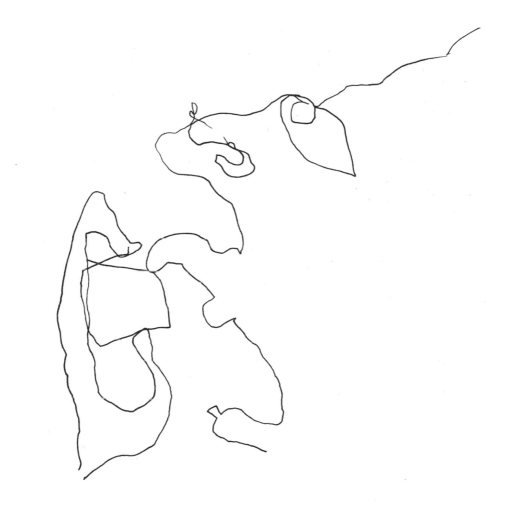

A WOMAN WHO HAS A TOUGH PILL TO SWALLOW

A WOMAN WHO FEELS GUILTY ABOUT FEELING ANGRY

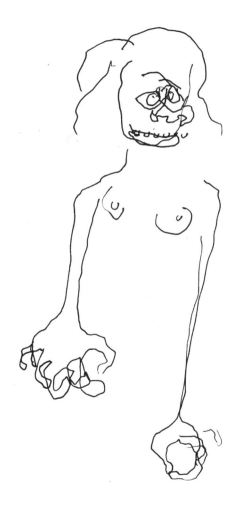

A WOMAN WHO IS TOO TIRED TO MOVE

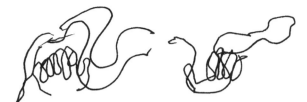

A WOMAN WHO TRIES TO USE HER SNAKE-
CHARMING ABILITIES TO GET HER SON HIGHER GRADES

A WOMAN WHO CAN'T REMEMBER WHY SHE LOVES
CHRISTMAS SO MUCH

A WOMAN WHO IN HER EFFORTS AT TOTAL RELAXATION
HAS SUCCEEDED TO SUCH A DEGREE THAT SHE IS
NO LONGER ABLE TO GO ON STAGE

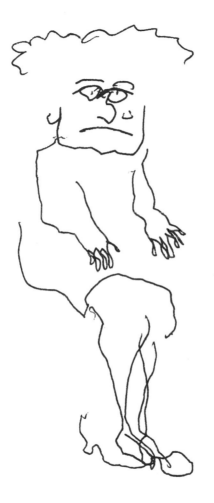

A   WOMAN WHO JUST REALIZED HER FEET ARE HOT

A WOMAN WHO IS CONSIDERING A BOOB LIFT

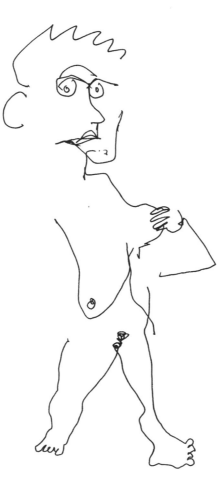

A WOMAN WHOSE INSANELY ROLLICKING DISPOSITION WAS
A BIG HIT WITH THE YOUNGER SET IN THE 1920'S BUT
NOW FRIGHTENS PASSERSBY ON FIFTH AVENUE

A WOMAN WHO LOVES TO DO THINGS FOR OTHERS AND
THEN RESENTS IT AFTERWARDS

A WOMAN WHO KNOWS SHE'S WRONG BUT IS FEELING
SORRY FOR HERSELF ANYWAY

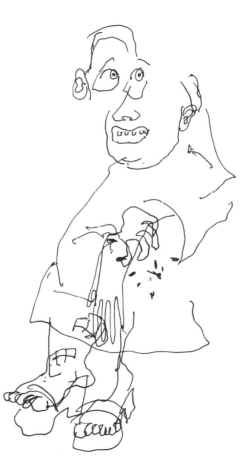

A WOMAN WHO STARTED GOING TO CHURCH AFTER HER SON
MARRIED A JEWISH GIRL

A WOMAN WHO IS NOT SURE WHETHER HER VISIONS
ARE COMING FROM GOD OR THE DEVIL

A WOMAN WHO IS SO FIXED ON HER OWN NEUROSES
THAT SHE NO LONGER NOTICES THE WORLD AROUND HER

A WOMAN WHO IS FLYING FOR THE FIRST TIME

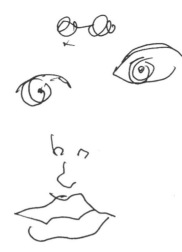

A Note on the Author

Rebecca Miller is the author of *Personal Velocity* (a *Washington Post* Best Book of 2001) and the acclaimed director of *Angela* and *Personal Velocity* (winner of a Grand Jury prize at the Sundance Film Festival in 2002).

Acknowledgments

Thank you Robert Younger, Michael Rohatyn, and Barbara Browning – the first friends to see these drawings and think they could be a book. And thanks to my agent, Sarah Chalfant, for her perseverance; to MaryAnn Camilleri, for her help; and to Karen Rinaldi, for publishing it.